P9-DGK-712

Garfield bigger than life

BY: JIM DAVIS

BALLANTINE BOOKS · NEW YORK

Sale of this book without a front cover may be unauthorized. If this book is coverless, it may have been reported to the publisher as "unsold or destroyed" and neither the author nor the publisher may have received payment for it.

Copyright © 1981 by United Feature Syndicate, Inc.

All rights reserved under International and Pan-American Copyright Conventions. Published in the United States by Ballantine Books, a division of Random House, Inc., New York, and simultaneously in Canada by Random House of Canada Limited, Toronto, Canada.

Library of Congress Catalog Card Number: 81-066659

ISBN 0-345-32007-7

Manufactured in the United States of America

First Ballantine Books Edition: November 1981

40 39 38

how to draw Garfield
1.
PASTA SPOTTERS
DAISY SNIFFER
2.
CAN OPENER SENSORS
SMIRK
SMIRK RETAINERS
3.
STROKING SURFACE
LASAGNA STORAGE UNITS
TWITCHER
4.
HAIR BALL CATCHER
DIRT DRAGGER
CHAIR SHREDDERS
5.
NOT JUST ANOTHER PRETTY FACE
STRIPES
NOW ADD THE PERSONALITY
JIM DAVIS

© 1979 United Feature Syndicate, Inc.

© 1979 United Feature Syndicate, Inc.
8-29

OH, GREAT

GARFIELD ATE MY TOOTHPASTE AGAIN
JIM DAVIS

I JUST LOVE TO COURT DANGER
8-30

SPLOOSH!

© 1979 United Feature Syndicate, Inc.
YIPEEE, HA-HA, WHEEE
JIM DAVIS

THIS IS MY PET ANT, LYLE. HE'S CUTE, QUIET, AND INDUSTRIOUS
8-31
JIM DAVIS

SPLAT!

THE "LATE" LYLE WAS ALSO EYEBALLING MY LASAGNA
© 1979 United Feature Syndicate, Inc.

9-1
© 1979 United Feature Syndicate, Inc.

WHAT ?! WHERE ?!

HE DID IT AGAIN
JIM DAVIS

SCUFFLE
SCUFFLE
STRUGGLE
GRAB!
STUFF
STUFF

GUESS WHAT, GARFIELD? WHILE MOM AND DAD'RE ON A WEEK'S VACATION, WE'RE GOING TO BABY-SIT FOR THEIR KITTEN
9-3

MEET NERMAL

WAKE ME IN A WEEK
© 1979 United Feature Syndicate, Inc.
JIM DAVIS

I GOTTA SPEND A WEEK WET-NURSING NERMAL, HERE... HE'S CUTE
9-4
© 1979 United Feature Syndicate, Inc.

AND I HATE "CUTE".
JIM DAVIS

DON'T KNOCK IT, JACK. I MAKE A KILLING POSING FOR GREETING CARDS

OKAY, NERMAL. THERE'S A DOG. ...KILL!
9-5
© 1979 United Feature Syndicate, Inc.

OH, NERMAL. NERMAL, NERMAL, NERMAL
JIM DAVIS

CRUD!
GARFIELD
9-6
© 1979 United Feature Syndicate, Inc.

NERMAL SHED ALL OVER MY FOOD
GARFIELD

I CAN'T STAND CAT HAIRS UNLESS THEY'RE MY OWN
GARFIELD
JIM DAVIS

© 1979 United Feature Syndicate, Inc.

9-7

9-8

© 1979 United Feature Syndicate, Inc.

SPLOOSH!
OH-NO! A VICIOUS UNDERTOW IS DRAGGING ME OUT TO SEA!
I'M TOO YOUNG TO GO!
9-9
I CAN SEE THE HEADLINES NOW... "WORLD FAMOUS CAT LOST AT SEA. MILLIONS OF BEAUTIFUL GIRL CATS GRIEF-STRICKEN!"
I CAN'T MAKE IT! I'M GOING DOWN FOR THE THIRD TIME!
© 1979 United Feature Syndicate, Inc.
I'D SAVE YOU, GARFIELD. BUT I'M NOT ABOUT TO GIVE A CAT MOUTH-TO-MOUTH RESUSCITATION
JIM DAVIS

9-10
YAWN
© 1979 United Feature Syndicate, Inc.

OH, THIS LOOKS LIKE A NICE PLACE TO SLEEP

IF YOU DON'T MIND, GARFIELD..
JIM DAVIS

SACK! PILLAGE! MAIM! DESTROY!
9-11

BONK!

WHIMPER, LIMP, CRY, HURT, MOAN
JIM DAVIS
© 1979 United Feature Syndicate, Inc.

IT'S TIME TO PUT YOUR LEASH ON FOR A NICE WALK
9-12

OH COME ON, GARFIELD. IT'S NOT THAT BAD

© 1979 United Feature Syndicate, Inc.
JIM DAVIS

I KNOW YOU DON'T LIKE YOUR LEASH, GARFIELD, BUT PEOPLE ARE STARING

SO CUT THAT OUT

JIM DAVIS
© 1979 United Feature Syndicate, Inc.
9-13

ODIE, YOU KNOW BETTER THAN THAT
© 1979 United Feature Syndicate, Inc.

DO YOU KNOW WHAT I APPRECIATE ABOUT YOU MOST, GARFIELD?
9-14

I'M HOUSEBROKEN
YOU'RE HOUSEBROKEN
JIM DAVIS

SOME PEOPLE SAY PETS ARE NOT CLEAN
© 1979 United Feature Syndicate, Inc.
9-15

THAT MAY BE SO

BUT TRY EATING YOUR NEXT MEAL WITHOUT YOUR HANDS AND SEE HOW WELL **YOU** FARE
JIM DAVIS

SMACK
MUNCH
SLURP

CLICK!
9-16

ZZZ

ZZZ
JIM DAVIS

I DIDN'T KNOW CATS COULD EAT IN THEIR SLEEP

BUT I DO KNOW THEY CAN'T SHARPEN THEIR CLAWS IN THEIR SLEEP
I SHOULDN'T HAVE PUSHED IT
© 1979 United Feature Syndicate, Inc.

ATTENTION AMERICA! I AM HEREBY DECLARING THIS WEEK **NATIONAL FAT WEEK**
© 1979 United Feature Syndicate, Inc.

THIS IS THE WEEK FOR ALL YOU FAT PEOPLE TO COME OUT OF THE CLOSET
9-17

THOSE OF YOU WHO COULD GET INTO ONE, THAT IS
JIM DAVIS

THIS IS NATIONAL FAT WEEK. I WANT TO HEAR ALL YOU FAT PEOPLE SAY, "I'M FAT, AND I'M PROUD OF IT!"
© 1979 United Feature Syndicate, Inc.
JIM DAVIS

LOUDER! "I'M FAT, AND I'M PROUD OF IT!"
9-18

YOU...THE PUDGY ONE IN SEATTLE, I DIDN'T HEAR YOU

HERE'S A NATIONAL FAT WEEK HANDY FAT TIP
© 1979 United Feature Syndicate, Inc.

"DON'T EXERCISE." YOU'LL BE HAPPIER

HAVE YOU EVER SEEN A JOGGER LAUGH?
9-19
JIM DAVIS

HERE'S A NATIONAL FAT WEEK SKINNY JOKE
9-20
JIM DAVIS

HOW MANY SKINNY PEOPLE DOES IT TAKE TO FILL A SHOWER?

I DON'T KNOW. THEY KEEP SLIPPING DOWN THE DRAIN
© 1979 United Feature Syndicate, Inc.

HERE'S THE NATIONAL FAT WEEK "WEIGHT-HEIGHT CHART"
© 1979 United Feature Syndicate, Inc.

ACCORDING TO THIS, IF YOU WEIGH 200 POUNDS, YOU SHOULD BE 6'4"
9-21

THAT MEANS IF YOU'RE UNDER 6'4" YOU'RE NOT OVERWEIGHT, YOU'RE UNDERTALL
JIM DAVIS

WELL, FAT BROTHERS AND SISTERS, THIS IS THE LAST DAY OF NATIONAL FAT WEEK
9-22

JUST REMEMBER, "ROUND IS BEAUTIFUL"

NOW GET OUT THERE AND EAT A CHICKEN FRANCHISE
JIM DAVIS
© 1979 United Feature Syndicate, Inc.

CARTOONIST'S NOTE: TODAY'S GARFIELD STRIP IS TO BE READ ONLY BY FAT PEOPLE, OR PEOPLE WITH FAT TENDENCIES. YOU SKINNY ONES CAN READ THE OTHER STRIPS, OR JOG, OR DRINK A GLASS OF WATER, OR WHATEVER IT IS SKINNY PEOPLE DO. ...I WOULDN'T KNOW.
I AM HEREBY DECLARING THIS COMING WEEK, "NATIONAL FAT WEEK"
OUT OF THE CLOSET, YOU FATTIES!
THIS WEEK WE'RE GOING TO EAT WITHOUT GUILT
© 1979 United Feature Syndicate, Inc.
9-23
REMEMBER OUR SLOGAN: "IF IT'S NOT DEEP-FRIED, IT'S NOT WORTH EATING."
WE'LL BOYCOTT CARROTS AND TELL SKINNY JOKES
I WOULD HAVE HAD A NATIONAL CONVENTION
BUT I COULDN'T GET THE KANSAS CITY STOCKYARDS TO CATER IT
JIM DAVIS

© 1979 United Feature Syndicate, Inc.

© 1979 United Feature Syndicate, Inc.

GARFIELD! BREAKFAST!
9-26

BONK!

I DID IT AGAIN. I GOT UP BEFORE I WOKE UP
© 1979 United Feature Syndicate, Inc.
JIM DAVIS

WAG WAG WAG
© 1979 United Feature Syndicate, Inc.

STOMP!

WAG WAG WAG
9-27
JIM DAVIS

© 1979 United Feature Syndicate, Inc.
9-28

MEYOW

LET ME GUESS. YOU WERE IN THE PICKLED HERRING AGAIN
JIM DAVIS

EAT UP, GARFIELD
MEYOW
GARFIELD
© 1979 United Feature Syndicate, Inc.
9-29

IT SAYS HERE THIS IS A "NEW IMPROVED" CAT FOOD
MUNCH MUNCH
GARFIELD

MEYOW!
GARFIELD
JIM DAVIS

9-30

OH, DARN

JON'S FLOWER GARDEN GOT A LITTLE OVER-FROLICKED
JIM DAVIS
© 1979 United Feature Syndicate, Inc.

© 1979 United Feature Syndicate, Inc.

© 1979 United Feature Syndicate, Inc.

BE RIGHT WITH YOU, MR. ARBUCKLE
© 1979 United Feature Syndicate, Inc.

I'LL BE HERE WITH BELLS ON, DOCTOR
THAT MAKES FOR AN INTERESTING MENTAL PICTURE

WHY DOES SHE ALWAYS PUT ME DOWN?
YOU'RE SO PUTDOWNABLE
10-3
JIM DAVIS

HOW ABOUT GOING OUT WITH ME, DOCTOR?
I WOULDN'T GO OUT WITH YOU IF YOU WERE THE LAST MAN ON EARTH
10-4

THEN HOW ABOUT SOMETIME AFTER THAT?
THAT'S A GOOD ONE
JIM DAVIS
© 1979 United Feature Syndicate, Inc.

WHY WON'T YOU GO OUT WITH ME, DOCTOR?
BECAUSE I HATE YOUR GUTS
10-5

DOES THIS MEAN MARRIAGE IS OUT OF THE QUESTION?
DON QUIXOTE STRIKES AGAIN
JIM DAVIS
© 1979 United Feature Syndicate, Inc.

HOW ABOUT A DATE, DOC?
NO WAY
10-6

MMMM

GREAT! SEE YOU AT EIGHT
IF YOU CAN'T CONVINCE'M, CONFUSE'M
JIM DAVIS
© 1979 United Feature Syndicate, Inc.

CAUTION
HMMM, WET CEMENT
SPLUT!
OOPS!
© 1979 United Feature Syndicate, Inc.
BARK! BARK!
SLURP
LASSIE WOULD HAVE GONE FOR HELP
JIM DAVIS
10-7

I SUPPOSE YOU WANT TO KNOW HOW MY DATE WENT WITH LIZ, THE VET...WELL DON'T ASK
I WON'T
10-8

SHE DIDN'T SHOW. OLD JON GOT STOOD UP
I DON'T WANT TO HEAR ABOUT IT

YOU KNOW, GARFIELD. I LIKE YOU BETTER THAN PEOPLE
TELL ME MORE
© 1979 United Feature Syndicate, Inc.
JIM DAVIS

MUNCH MUNCH MUNCH
10-9

SMACK! SLURP! GOBBLE!

© 1979 United Feature Syndicate, Inc.
JIM DAVIS

MY AUNT EVELYN IS THE NEATEST CAT I KNOW
© 1979 United Feature Syndicate, Inc.
10-10

SHE PLUCKED ALL THE HAIR OFF HER BODY SO SHE WOULDN'T SHED ON THE FURNITURE

NOW SHE'S LIVING WITH A FAMILY IN L.A. THAT THINKS SHE'S A CHIHUAHUA
JIM DAVIS

YIP! YIP! YIP!
© 1979 United Feature Syndicate, Inc.

YIP! YIP! YIP!

FOR THE LAST TIME, ODIE, YOU CHASE THE TAIL
JIM DAVIS
10-11

GARFIELD, MUST YOU DO EVERYTHING I DO?
10-12

THAT WASN'T VERY NICE

AFTER ALL, CATS ARE JUST LITTLE PEOPLE WITH FUR AND FANGS
JIM DAVIS
© 1979 United Feature Syndicate, Inc.

© 1979 United Feature Syndicate, Inc.
10-13

FWIP
FWIP
FWIP
FWIP
FWIP
FWIP
SHOOP!

A VENETIAN TONGUE
JIM DAVIS

WAKE UP, SLEEPYHEAD!
WE'RE HAVING BREAKFAST ON THE PATIO THIS MORNING
BECAUSE I WANT TO SHARE THIS BEAUTIFUL SUNRISE WITH YOU
10-14
JIM DAVIS
WHERE ELSE CAN YOU FIND A LIVING, BREATHING WORK OF ART CREATED JUST FOR YOU? FRESH WITH THE PROMISE OF A BRIGHT NEW DAY
HAVE YOU EVER SEEN A MORE GLORIOUS SIGHT, GARFIELD?.. UH, GARFIELD?
© 1979 United Feature Syndicate, Inc.
GET YOUR FACE OUT OF THE SCRAMBLED EGGS, GARFIELD
ZZZZ

© 1979 United Feature Syndicate, Inc.

© 1979 United Feature Syndicate, Inc.

SOAP
© 1979 United Feature Syndicate, Inc.
10-17

SOAP

CATS!
SOAP
JIM DAVIS

10-18

ZIP!!

© 1979 United Feature Syndicate, Inc.
FOUL! FOUL! NO FAIR! FOUL!
SOAP
JIM DAVIS

MORNIN'
GOOD MORNING, IRMA
10-19

THE COFFEE'S STRONG, HON. YOU'D BETTER GET IT BEFORE IT GETS YOU
IS IT HOT?
© 1979 United Feature Syndicate, Inc.

YUP
THIS ISN'T ONE OF YOUR BETTER DINERS
JIM DAVIS

MY, YOU LOOK NICE TODAY, IRMA
ARE YOU KIDDING?
10-20

WHEN I COME TO WORK I WEAR BASE AND LIPSTICK AND THAT'S IT, HON. I DON'T PUT ON EYES UNLESS I HAVE A HOT DATE. YOU KNOW WHAT I MEAN?
© 1979 United Feature Syndicate, Inc.

I DIDN'T EVEN SHAVE MY LEGS
THIS DEFINITELY ISN'T ONE OF YOUR BETTER DINERS
JIM DAVIS

© 1979 United Feature Syndicate, Inc.

© 1979 United Feature Syndicate, Inc.

SMACK!
10-22

I HATE PATIO DOORS
JIM DAVIS

10-23
© 1979 United Feature Syndicate, Inc.

HEY, GARFIELD, WHERE'S ODIE?
HE'S EASY ENOUGH TO FIND

JIM DAVIS
JUST FOLLOW THE SLOBBER

© 1979 United Feature Syndicate, Inc.

YOU MAY HAVE THE LEFTOVERS WHEN I'M THROUGH, GARFIELD
© 1979 United Feature Syndicate, Inc.

KONG!

YOU DON'T HAVE TO BE PATIENT WHEN YOU'RE AS BIG AS I AM
10-26
JIM DAVIS

ARE YOU STILL HAVING BREAKFAST ?
GARFIELD
10-27
© 1979 United Feature Syndicate, Inc.

YOU'VE SPENT AN HOUR EATING YOUR CEREAL
GARFIELD

YOU KNOW I DON'T LIKE RAISINS
GARFIELD
JIM DAVIS

SLIT!
10-28
© 1979 United Feature Syndicate, Inc.
MUNCH
SMACK
SLURP
PTOOEY!
BURP
GARFIELD WENT TO SO MUCH TROUBLE I HATED TO SPOIL IT FOR HIM
JIM DAVIS

GOOD BOY, GARFIELD. GIVE ME THE PAPER
© 1979 United Feature Syndicate, Inc.
10-29

EITHER I GET BREAKFAST OR YOU'LL NEVER SEE THIS PAPER ALIVE AGAIN

WHY IS THERE ALWAYS A STRING ATTACHED?!
NOTHING'S FREE, PAL
JIM DAVIS

© 1979 United Feature Syndicate, Inc.

FLIP!

JIM DAVIS
I CAN TAKE A HINT
10-30

I HAVE SOME-THING FOR THAT APPETITE OF YOURS, GARFIELD
© 1979 United Feature Syndicate, Inc.

CLOSE YOUR EYES AND OPEN YOUR MOUTH

JIM DAVIS
10-31

HERE'S A HANDY HINT FOR YOU BACHELORS OUT THERE
© 1979 United Feature Syndicate, Inc.

YOU CAN KEEP YOUR LAUNDRY DETERGENT DRY

BY SEALING IT IN A COOKIE JAR
11-1
JIM DAVIS

© 1979 United Feature Syndicate, Inc.

© 1979 United Feature Syndicate, Inc.

MUNCH MUNCH MUNCH
GARFIELD
WHEW! I COULDN'T EAT ANOTHER BITE
GARFIELD
GARFIELD
RRRR
GARFIELD
11-4
ROWR
GARFIELD
RRR
GARFIELD
GARFIELD
GARFIELD
© 1979 United Feature Syndicate, Inc.
JIM DAVIS

PACK YOUR BAGS, GARFIELD. WE'RE GOING ON VACATION
© 1979 United Feature Syndicate, Inc.
11-5

GOOD IDEA

I COULD USE THE REST
JIM DAVIS

WE HAVE A LONG WAY TO GO, GARFIELD
JIM DAVIS

I WISH YOU ENJOYED RIDING IN A CAR MORE
© 1979 United Feature Syndicate, Inc.

YOU'RE TOO TENSE
11-6

I'D LIKE A ROOM FOR THE NIGHT
© 1979 United Feature Syndicate, Inc.
11-7

ANY PETS?
NOPE

JIM DAVIS

© 1979 United Feature Syndicate, Inc. JIM DAVIS

LOOK AT THAT, GARFIELD. WHAT DO YOU...
11-8

...UH, THINK

11-9

© 1979 United Feature Syndicate, Inc.

11-10

© 1979 United Feature Syndicate, Inc.

POKE!
GRRRRRR
CHOKE!
GASP!
KICK!
KONG!
JIM DAVIS
© 1979 United Feature Syndicate, Inc.

rain (rān) n. 1. water falling to earth in drops

11/12
2. a mild depressant
JIM DAVIS
© 1979 United Feature Syndicate, Inc.

© 1979 United Feature Syndicate, Inc.
ZZZZ

SCREECH!

CHASING CARS AGAIN, GARFIELD?
JIM DAVIS
11-13

WHY ARE WE PLACED ON THIS EARTH? WHAT IS OUR PURPOSE? WHAT IS OUR MISSION IN LIFE?
© 1979 United Feature Syndicate, Inc.

THANK YOU SO MUCH FOR YOUR PROMPT REPLY
11-14
JIM DAVIS

11-15
© 1979 United Feature Syndicate, Inc.

JIM DAVIS
NICE TRY, HOT SHOT

HOW'S YOUR COFFEE, HON?
IT'S A BIT STRONG

SAY IT'S NOT SO! SAY IT'S NOT SO! I COULD JUST SHOOT MYSELF!
11-16

YOU USUALLY DON'T FIND ONE THAT DEDICATED
IT'S HER LIFE
© 1979 United Feature Syndicate, Inc.
JIM DAVIS

11-17
I HATE IT WHEN GARFIELD FALLS ASLEEP IN MY LAP
ZZZ

HE SNUGGLES UP
ZZZ

AND DIGS IN
ZZZ
© 1979 United Feature Syndicate, Inc.
JIM DAVIS

BOING!
BOING!
JIM DAVIS
© 1979 United Feature Syndicate, Inc.

MUNCH
MUNCH
MUNCH
GARFIELD

CLOBBER!
GARFIELD

LOVE IS A
FICKLE THING
GARFIELD
11-18

© 1979 United Feature Syndicate, Inc.

IT'S TIME YOU STARTED TAKING VITAMINS, GARFIELD
NO WAY, PAL. MY BODY'S A TEMPLE
© 1979 United Feature Syndicate, Inc.
11-21

I PUT THEM IN THIS LASAGNA

EVEN A TEMPLE NEEDS HIS VITAMIN C
JIM DAVIS

DOESN'T IT BOTHER YOU THAT YOUR CAT IS ALWAYS UNDERFOOT?

NOT AT ALL. GARFIELD IS VERY FOND OF ME
© 1979 United Feature Syndicate, Inc.

11-22
WE'RE INSEPARABLE, AREN'T WE, GARFIELD?
YOU'RE STANDING ON MY TAIL
JIM DAVIS

I OFTEN WONDER WHAT GOES ON IN THAT COMPLEX MIND OF YOURS, GARFIELD
BZZZZZZZZZZZZZ

WOULDN'T IT BE WONDERFUL IF HUMANS AND ANIMALS COULD COMMUNICATE?
SMACK!
JIM DAVIS
© 1979 United Feature Syndicate, Inc.

WHAT WOULD YOU SAY TO ME IF YOU COULD TALK RIGHT NOW?
I JUST KILLED A FLY SOMEWHERE ON YOUR RAISIN TOAST
11-23

THAT'S A NASTY COLD YOU HAVE THERE, GARFIELD
SNIFF
© 1979 United Feature Syndicate, Inc.

WE'LL TAKE YOU TO THE VET AND GET YOU FIXED RIGHT UP
JIM DAVIS

NEVER SAY "FIXED" TO AN ANIMAL PERSON
11-24

THERE'S NOTHING LIKE A BRISK MORNING JOG IN THERMAL UNDERWEAR
HMMM. A THREAD
© 1979 United Feature Syndicate, Inc.
11-25
JIM DAVIS
SLAM
VERY FUNNY, GARFIELD

© 1979 United Feature Syndicate, Inc.

© 1979 United Feature Syndicate, Inc.

© 1979 United Feature Syndicate, Inc.

© 1979 United Feature Syndicate, Inc.

© 1979 United Feature Syndicate, Inc.

© 1979 United Feature Syndicate, Inc.

© 1979 United Feature Syndicate, Inc.

© 1979 United Feature Syndicate, Inc.

HOW CUTE!
HOP
HOP
HOP
© 1979 United Feature Syndicate, Inc.

BOOM!
BOOM!
BOOM!

SOMEHOW, GARFIELD, YOUR GRASP OF "CUTE" IS A LITTLE SHAKY
12-5
JIM DAVIS

SCRATCH!
SCRATCH!
SCRATCH!
SCRATCH!
© 1979 United Feature Syndicate, Inc.
JIM DAVIS

THERE'S ONE NICE THING ABOUT HAVING ANOTHER CAT AROUND THE HOUSE
12-6

NERMAL!

I'M TIRED OF COMPETING WITH THAT NERMAL. I THINK I'LL GIVE HIM A GOOD POUNDING TODAY
© 1979 United Feature Syndicate, Inc.

WHERE IS THAT LITTLE FUZZBALL? HE COULD BE ANYWHERE
GARFIELD

GARFIELD
12-7
JIM DAVIS

IT'S TIME WE DETERMINED WHO'S MASTER OF THIS HOUSEHOLD
12-8
© 1979 United Feature Syndicate, Inc.

SMACK!

HOW DID HE DO THAT?
T*
JIM DAVIS

© 1979 United Feature Syndicate, Inc.

© 1979 United Feature Syndicate, Inc.

JIM DAVIS

IT'S TIME WE TALKED ABOUT THIS COFFEE DEPENDENCY OF YOURS, GARFIELD
AHHH
12-10

PLIP!
© 1979 United Feature Syndicate, Inc.

HOT! HOT! HOT! HOT!

JIM DAVIS
12-11

© 1979 United Feature Syndicate, Inc.
JIM DAVIS

GET OFF THE PIANO, ODIE. YOU'RE MAKING TOO MUCH RACKET

12·12
AND YOU...

GARFIELD! THAT'S BEAUTIFUL!

WE'LL GO ON THE ROAD. WE'LL MAKE A MILLION! WE'RE RICH!

© 1979 United Feature Syndicate, Inc.
JIM DAVIS
12·13

STOP PLAYING WITH THE FLASHLIGHT, GARFIELD
CLICK!
© 1979 United Feature Syndicate, Inc.
12-14
JIM DAVIS

JIM DAVIS
YOUR PICTURE 4 FOR 50¢
12-15
© 1979 United Feature Syndicate, Inc.

LET'S GO LOOK AT NEW FURNITURE, GARFIELD

FURNITURE CITY
GEE, THIS SOFA'S NICE. WHAT DO YOU THINK, GARFIELD?

GARFIELD?
© 1979 United Feature Syndicate, Inc.

POW!

KOOOOSH
POP!
POP!
SSSSSS
POW!
PLIF

CONGRATULATIONS, SIR. YOU ARE NOW THE PROUD OWNER OF 23 SLIGHTLY CLAWED INFLATABLE CHAIRS
I HAVEN'T HAD SO MUCH FUN SINCE GRANNY GOT HER TAIL CAUGHT IN THE WRINGER
JIM DAVIS

12-16

© 1979 United Feature Syndicate, Inc.

© 1979 United Feature Syndicate, Inc.

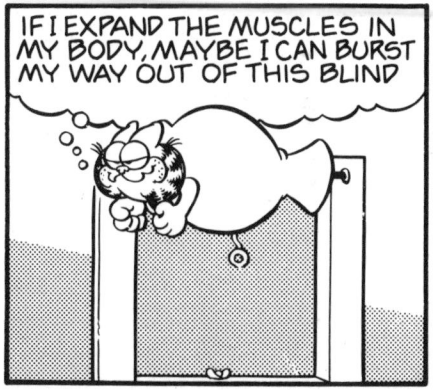
IF I EXPAND THE MUSCLES IN MY BODY, MAYBE I CAN BURST MY WAY OUT OF THIS BLIND

DRAT! I FORGOT
12-19

WHAT MUSCLES?
JIM DAVIS
© 1979 United Feature Syndicate, Inc.

12-20

JIM DAVIS
I WAS AFRAID OF THAT
© 1979 United Feature Syndicate, Inc.

12-21
JIM DAVIS
HEY, GARFIELD

WHAT ARE YOU DOING UP THERE?

IN A WORLD FULL OF IDIOTS, I GET THE GRAND HIGH LLAMA
© 1979 United Feature Syndicate, Inc.

JIM DAVIS
LET ME GET YOU OUT OF THAT BLIND, GARFIELD
© 1979 United Feature Syndicate, Inc.

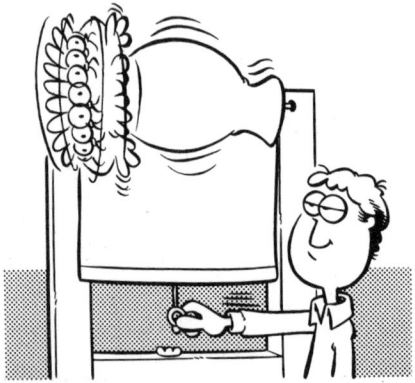

12-22

© 1979 United Feature Syndicate, Inc.
JIM DAVIS
UH-OH! HERE COMES JON!
THE PERFECT CRIME
OH, GARFIELD
HAVE YOU, PERCHANCE, SEEN MY CHICKEN?
12-23

12-24

© 1979 United Feature Syndicate, Inc.

© 1979 United Feature Syndicate, Inc.

I FROZE A SPECIAL TREAT FOR YOU, GARFIELD

OH, GOODY
12-26

CAT FOOD ON A STICK
JIM DAVIS
© 1979 United Feature Syndicate, Inc.

IT'S TRUE CATS ALWAYS LAND ON THEIR FEET

12-27

THE THINGS I DO FOR THIS STRIP
© 1979 United Feature Syndicate, Inc.
JIM DAVIS

© 1979 United Feature Syndicate, Inc.
12-28

SPIDERS ARE CURIOUS INSECTS TO SEE. THEIR WEBS ARE REALLY NEAT.

BUT HOW DO THEY WEAVE THEM ELABORATELY, WHEN ALL THEY HAVE IS FEET?
JIM DAVIS

GARFIELD AND I CAN ACTUALLY COMMUNICATE. WATCH THIS...

WOULD YOU LIKE TO TAKE A BATH, GARFIELD?
12-29

GARFIELD SAID "NO"
© 1979 United Feature Syndicate, Inc.
JIM DAVIS

CRASH!

GARFIELD! YOU BROKE MY FERN !!
© 1979 United Feature Syndicate, Inc.

I RAISED THAT FERN FROM A FROND!
12-30

WHAT DID THAT FERN EVER DO TO YOU ?!!

WHY, I HAVE A NOTION TO...UH...TO

I...UH

YOU'RE SO CUTE
LIKE PUTTY IN MY PAWS
JIM DAVIS

THIS YEAR I RESOLVE TO LOSE WEIGHT...
12-31

TO BE NICER TO DOGS...

AND TO SPROUT WINGS AND FLY
JIM DAVIS
© 1979 United Feature Syndicate, Inc.

SO THIS IS 1980
© 1980 United Feature Syndicate, Inc.
1-1

FEELS ABOUT THE SAME
JIM DAVIS

YOU'RE A SWELL CAT, GARFIELD
© 1980 United Feature Syndicate, Inc.
1-2

IT'S TIME WE DID MORE THINGS TOGETHER

LIKE GIVE YOU A BATH!
I KNEW IT! I KNEW IT!
JIM DAVIS

DARN THE TORPEDOES! FULL SPEED AHEAD!
© 1980 United Feature Syndicate, Inc.
1-3

NEVER HAVE SO FEW GIVEN SO MUCH TO SO MANY

QUIT DAWDLING, GARFIELD
HOW DARE YOU SPEAK THAT WAY TO THE PRESIDENT OF THE UNITED STATES
JIM DAVIS

© 1980 United Feature Syndicate, Inc.

BACK OFF, GARFIELD. THAT TURKEY LEG IS FOR MY LUNCH

AHCHOO!

WIPE
WIPE
WIPE
WIPE

SCRATCH
SCRATCH
SCRATCH
SCRATCH
SCRATCH
SCRATCH
© 1980 United Feature Syndicate, Inc
1-6

WOULD YOU LIKE A TURKEY LEG, GARFIELD ?
ONLY IF YOU DON'T WANT IT
JIM DAVIS

SLURP!
© 1980 United Feature Syndicate, Inc

THE COFFEE'S TOO HOT, GARFIELD

THANKS FOR TELLING ME
JIM DAVIS
1-7

WHAT WOULD YOU LIKE FOR BREAKFAST, GARFIELD?
SOMETHING DIFFERENT!
© 1980 United Feature Syndicate, Inc.
1-8

THE USUAL, YOU SAY?
NO! NO! NO! NO! NO! NO!

ONE USUAL COMING UP!
IT'S THINGS LIKE THIS THAT CONTRIBUTE TO THE HIGH SUICIDE RATE AMONG CATS
GARFIELD
JIM DAVIS

YIP!
PUNT!

© 1980 United Feature Syndicate, Inc.
1-9
JIM DAVIS

THROW ME A ROLL, JON
© 1980 United Feature Syndicate, Inc.

GULP!

1-10

PASS ME A ROLL, JON
JIM DAVIS

© 1980 United Feature Syndicate, Inc.

© 1980 United Feature Syndicate, Inc.

1-13
I THOUGHT SO
© 1980 United Feature Syndicate, Inc.
JIM DAVIS

SNIFF
1-14

OH DOE! I'M CUBBING DOWN WID A CODE

LOOG, I CAN HARDLY EBBEN UNDERSTAD BY OWN THOUGHTS
JIM DAVIS
© 1980 United Feature Syndicate, Inc.

SNIFF
© 1980 United Feature Syndicate, Inc.
1-15

OH, ICKY POO! GARFIELD'S GOT A COLD. HE'S DISEASED! EVERYONE STAND BACK!

BERRY FUDDY
JIM DAVIS

AH-CHOO!
© 1980 United Feature Syndicate, Inc.
1-16

IT'S YOURS, GARFIELD

THIS COULD BE THE START OF SOMETHING GRAND
JIM DAVIS

I HATE CODES
SNIFF
© 1980 United Feature Syndicate, Inc.
1-17

I CAN'T BELEEB HOW MUCH MY HEAD IS STUFFED UBB

JIM DAVIS

SNIFF
© 1980 United Feature Syndicate, Inc.
1-18

ARRRGH!!!

COLDS CAN BE FRUSTRATING CAN'T THEY, OL' BUDDY?
JIM DAVIS

YOUR COUGH SOUNDS BETTER, GARFIELD
HACK HACK
© 1980 United Feature Syndicate, Inc.

IT SHOULD
1-19

I'VE BEEN PRACTICING ALL NIGHT
JIM DAVIS

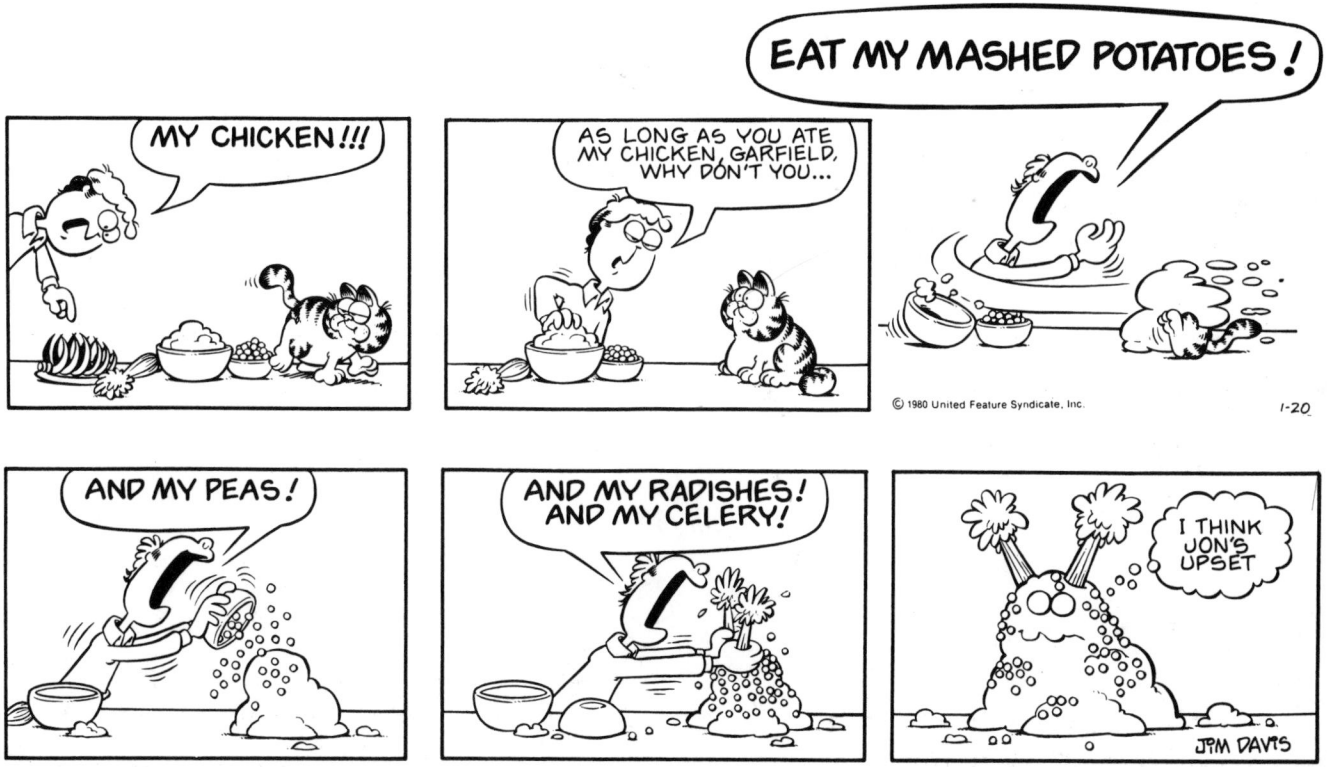

© 1980 United Feature Syndicate, Inc.

I LOVE A CHEERY FIRE IN A FIREPLACE
© 1980 United Feature Syndicate, Inc.
1-21

FOOMP!

IT'S THE SPARKS I'M NOT TOO FOND OF
JIM DAVIS

GARFIELD! LUNCH TIME!
1-22

I HATE IT WHEN MY FEET GO TO SLEEP
JIM DAVIS
© 1980 United Feature Syndicate, Inc.

FRANK, MEET GARFIELD
HI, GARFIELD
JIM DAVIS
1-23

ROWRRRR!

SOME PEOPLE RUB ME THE WRONG WAY
© 1980 United Feature Syndicate, Inc.

LET'S TALK ABOUT DOGS... WHAT ARE DOGS ?
© 1980 United Feature Syndicate, Inc.

1-24

ARE THEY VEGETABLE OR MINERAL ?
JIM DAVIS

GARÇON, I'LL HAVE THE ESCARGOT AND TRUFFLES FOR AN APPETIZER, THEN THE DUCK À L'ORANGE FLAMBÉ AND SOME CAPPUCCINO
JIM DAVIS
© 1980 United Feature Syndicate, Inc.

EAT UP, PAL
GARFIELD

TALK ABOUT LOWERING ONE'S SIGHTS...
GARFIELD
1-25

HERE'S YOUR COFFEE, HON

CRASH!
1-26

THIS ROLLER SKATING CRAZE IS GETTING OUT OF HAND
© 1980 United Feature Syndicate, Inc.
JIM DAVIS

LET'S TIGHTEN THAT LEASH, GARFIELD
I HATE LEASHES
FFT!
ROWR!
DON'T WORRY, GARFIELD. SOME KIND PASSER-BY WILL UNTIE US
1-27
UH, SIR? PARDON ME MA'AM... HEY YOU THERE... UH...
SLAM
HI, JON
HI, LYMAN
WHAT TOOK YOU SO LONG?
I HAD TO DRAG MYSELF HOME WITH MY LIPS
© 1980 United Feature Syndicate, Inc.
JIM DAVIS

MORNING, LIZ. JON HERE. I'M BRINGING GARFIELD IN FOR A CHECKUP TODAY
© 1980 United Feature Syndicate, Inc.

I KNOW YOU'VE BEEN WANTING TO GET TO KNOW ME BETTER, SO WHY DON'T YOU MAKE IT A LATE APPOINTMENT AND WE'LL GO TO DINNER AFTERWARD
1-28

JON... JON ARBUCKLE
JIM DAVIS

HI, DOCTOR! REMEMBER ME? JON? YOUR KNIGHT IN SHINING ARMOR?
© 1980 United Feature Syndicate, Inc.
1-29

OH YES, I REMEMBER

NAMES ESCAPE ME, BUT I NEVER FORGET A TWIT
JIM DAVIS

© 1980 United Feature Syndicate, Inc.

© 1980 United Feature Syndicate, Inc.

SAY, "AH," GARFIELD
2-1

I'LL TAKE YOUR TEMPERATURE IF YOU DON'T SAY, "AH"

AH
JIM DAVIS
© 1980 United Feature Syndicate, Inc.

I KNOW YOU'RE JUST A VETERINARIAN, LIZ, BUT I'VE HAD THESE DIZZY SPELLS LATELY...
2-2

WELL NOW, WHY DON'T WE JUST CHECK YOUR BLOOD PRESSURE

UH... DOCTOR
JIM DAVIS
© 1980 United Feature Syndicate, Inc.

OH BOY, IS IT CHILLY THIS MORNING
SPLASH SPLASH SPLASH
SIP
GARGLE GARGLE GARGLE
© 1980 United Feature Syndicate, Inc.
GULP
THAT FEELS SO WARM
AHHH
JIM DAVIS
YOU REALLY ENJOY YOUR COFFEE, DON'T YOU, GARFIELD?
2-3

READY FOR TENNIS?
AS SOON AS I FEED GARFIELD. HE'S HUNGRY
JIM DAVIS

HOW DO YOU KNOW THAT?
2-4

I HAVE MY WAYS
© 1980 United Feature Syndicate, Inc.

HERE'S A PICTURE OF GARFIELD AT THE ZOO
© 1980 United Feature Syndicate, Inc.
2-5

HERE'S GARFIELD SITTING NEXT TO A VERY RARE $ 300 PARROT

HERE'S A PICTURE OF ME SHELLING OUT 300 BUCKS FOR GARFIELD'S LUNCH
JIM DAVIS

HELP YOURSELF, GARFIELD
2-6

WOULD YOU LIKE A LITTLE COFFEE IN THAT SUGAR ?
JIM DAVIS
© 1980 United Feature Syndicate, Inc.

THIS SHOULD BLOW JON'S MIND. ME, GARFIELD, BEING NICE TO ODIE
PAT PAT
2-7

HEH HEH, HOW NICE
PAT PAT

THAT WAS A JOKE, YOU TWIT
JIM DAVIS
© 1980 United Feature Syndicate, Inc.

© 1980 United Feature Syndicate, Inc.
2-8

PUSH!

THIS TABLE WASN'T BIG ENOUGH FOR THE BOTH OF US
JIM DAVIS

POOMP!
JIM DAVIS 2-9

OOPS. I CRUNCHED JON'S ANTENNA

© 1980 United Feature Syndicate, Inc.
A LITTLE MORE TO THE RIGHT, GARFIELD

WATCH THIS. I'M GOING TO SWING DOWN ON THIS VINE AND SWOOP UP JON'S CHICKEN
YANK YANK
SWOOP!
JIM DAVIS
WHERE DID THE VINE COME FROM?
© 1980 United Feature Syndicate, Inc.
2-10

GUESS WHAT, GARFIELD? THIS WEEK WE'RE GOING TO VISIT DAD AND MOM ON THE FARM
© 1980 United Feature Syndicate, Inc.
2-11

YIPEE SKIP

I THINK I'LL CALL IN SICK THIS WEEK
JIM DAVIS

THERE'S ONLY ONE THING YOU HAVE TO REMEMBER WHEN WE GET TO THE FARM, GARFIELD

WATCH WHERE YOU STEP
2-12

© 1980 United Feature Syndicate, Inc.
JIM DAVIS
LET ME OUT

© 1980 United Feature Syndicate, Inc.

© 1980 United Feature Syndicate, Inc. JIM DAVIS

HOW'S GARFIELD ADJUSTING TO THE FARM?
JIM DAVIS 2-15

© 1980 United Feature Syndicate, Inc.
OINK!

YOU MEAN, HOW'S THE FARM ADJUSTING TO GARFIELD

I'M GLAD WE VISITED THE FARM, DAD
YUP
© 1980 United Feature Syndicate, Inc.

IT'S NICE TO GET AWAY FROM IT ALL
YUP

WAY, WAY, WAYYYY AWAY
JIM DAVIS 2-16

© 1980 United Feature Syndicate, Inc.
2-17
JIM DAVIS

THIS WOULD BE A GOOD MORNING FOR A BRISK WALK
JIM DAVIS
2-18

TO THE FOOD DISH
© 1980 United Feature Syndicate, Inc.

© 1980 United Feature Syndicate, Inc.
2-19

CLACK!

LIFE WASN'T HALF AS MUCH FUN BEFORE I GOT MY YO-YO BONE
JIM DAVIS

THE CAPED AVENGER SEES AN EVIL DOG

THE CAPED AVENGER SPRINGS INTO ACTION
2-20

JIM DAVIS
THE CAPED AVENGER HURTS HIMSELF
© 1980 United Feature Syndicate, Inc.

2-21
© 1980 United Feature Syndicate, Inc.

SWIPE!

THANKS, GARFIELD. I HATE TO LICK STAMPS
BLUH, BLUH
JIM DAVIS

© 1980 United Feature Syndicate, Inc.

© 1980 United Feature Syndicate, Inc.

© 1980 United Feature Syndicate, Inc.

IT'S NOT THE HAVING, IT'S THE GETTING
2-24
JIM DAVIS

YOU'RE TOO FAT, GARFIELD. I'M PUTTING YOU ON ANOTHER DIET
2-25

HE MAKES ME SO MAD

IF I COULD HAVE GOTTEN UP ON THAT CHAIR, I WOULD HAVE GIVEN HIM THE BEATING OF HIS LIFE
JIM DAVIS
© 1980 United Feature Syndicate, Inc.

HERE'S A CARROT FOR YOUR DIET, GARFIELD. YOU KNOW WHAT TO DO WITH IT
2-26

I CERTAINLY DO
JIM DAVIS

HERE RABBIT, RABBIT, RABBIT
© 1980 United Feature Syndicate, Inc.

I KNOW YOU'RE UNHAPPY, GARFIELD, BUT I WOULDN'T HAVE TO PUT YOU ON DIETS IF YOU WOULDN'T EAT SO MUCH
© 1980 United Feature Syndicate, Inc.
2-27

I CAN'T HELP IT. I HAVE A GLANDULAR CONDITION...

AN OVERACTIVE MOUTH GLAND
JIM DAVIS

THIS DIET'S A REAL BUMMER. I'M GETTING WEAKER BY THE MINUTE
© 1980 United Feature Syndicate, Inc.
2-28

I MUST BE GOING INTO CHOLESTEROL WITHDRAWAL

THAT'S WHEN YOU HAVE THE URGE TO MAKE A HIGHBALL OUT OF BACON GREASE
JIM DAVIS

© 1980 United Feature Syndicate, Inc.

OH NO, YOU DON'T, GARFIELD. THIS CHICKEN LEG IS MINE
3-2
LET'S HEAR IT FOR CLAWS
JIM DAVIS
© 1980 United Feature Syndicate, Inc.

GEE, I FEEL GOOD
© 1980 United Feature Syndicate, Inc.
3-3

I FEEL LIKE BEING NICE TO EVERYBODY TODAY

I MUST BE COMING DOWN WITH SOMETHING
JIM DAVIS

HEH HEH
3-4

CATS LOVE TO PLAY IN GROCERY BAGS

DARN... NO GROCERIES
© 1980 United Feature Syndicate, Inc.
JIM DAVIS

WHEN THE NEWSPAPER COMES EACH DAY, I TAKE THE EDITORIAL PAGE AND JON TAKES THE FUNNIES
© 1980 United Feature Syndicate, Inc.
3-5

HA! HA! HA! HA!

THERE'S NO ACCOUNTING FOR SOME PEOPLE'S TASTE
JIM DAVIS

JIM DAVIS
3-6

SWIPE!

LET ME GUESS... YOU'RE HUNGRY
RIGHT ON
© 1980 United Feature Syndicate, Inc.

COME ON, KITTY. SING YOUR SONG
3-7

DOO-DA, DOO-DA
JIM DAVIS
© 1980 United Feature Syndicate, Inc.

OH NO!
© 1980 United Feature Syndicate, Inc.
3-8

PUNT!

DON'T LAUGH. HOW WOULD YOU LIKE TO HAVE DOG DROOL ALL OVER YOUR TEDDY BEAR?
JIM DAVIS

© 1980 United Feature Syndicate, Inc.
3-9
GRACEFUL
BLOW IT OUT YOUR EAR
JIM DAVIS

THIS LOOKS LIKE IT'S GOING TO BE A GOOD WEEK
JIM DAVIS
© 1980 United Feature Syndicate, Inc.

NUTS... NUTS, NUTS, NUTS
3-10

MEYOW
© 1980 United Feature Syndicate, Inc.
3-11

LISTEN TO THAT
PURRR

THE KID'S A WALKING CLICHÉ
FFFT
JIM DAVIS

WHIP!
© 1980 United Feature Syndicate, Inc.
JIM DAVIS

RIP
RIP
RIP

AWW, HOW CUTE
3-12

GARFIELD, YOU SHOULD LEARN TO PLAY WITH NERMAL
SURE THING
HOP HOP
© 1980 United Feature Syndicate, Inc.

3-13

LET ME REPHRASE THAT
DRIBBLE DRIBBLE DRIBBLE
JIM DAVIS

JIM DAVIS
3-14

HERE, NERMAL. DO SOMETHING MORE CONSTRUCTIVE WITH YOUR TIME

© 1980 United Feature Syndicate, Inc.

SAY GOOD-BYE TO GARFIELD, NERMAL
SMACK
JIM DAVIS
© 1980 United Feature Syndicate, Inc.

3-15

© 1980 United Feature Syndicate, Inc.
3-16
ZIP!
WHERE THERE'S A WILL...
JIM DAVIS

GARFIELD, GET YOUR LAZY BONES OUT OF BED AND COME TO BREAKFAST
GARFIELD
JIM DAVIS
© 1980 United Feature Syndicate, Inc.

SCRAPE
SCRAPE
SCRAPE
GARFIELD

SCRAPE
SCRAPE
SCRAPE
GARFIELD
3-17

© 1980 United Feature Syndicate, Inc.
3-18

IS THAT ALL I AM TO YOU?
MERELY AN OBSTRUCTION IN THE ROAD OF LIFE
JIM DAVIS

I KNOW YOU CATS ARE INQUISITIVE BY NATURE, GARFIELD
© 1980 United Feature Syndicate, Inc.

AND I KNOW THIS IS YOUR HOME AS WELL AS MINE . . .

BUT STAY OUT OF MY UNDERWEAR DRAWER!!
3-19
JIM DAVIS

COMPUTERS... EVERYTHING IS CONTROLLED BY COMPUTERS THESE DAYS
© 1980 United Feature Syndicate, Inc.

THAT CHICKEN YOU ATE WAS EVEN RAISED BY A COMPUTER

3-20

burp
JIM DAVIS

LET'S GO EAT, ODIE
3-21

WHAT SAY YOU GO FORMAL

WITH A WHITE TIE AND TAIL
© 1980 United Feature Syndicate, Inc.
JIM DAVIS

IT'S A MYTH THAT CATS ARE HIGH-STRUNG
© 1980 United Feature Syndicate, Inc.
3-22

BARK

THERE'S A LOT OF TRUTH IN THOSE OLD MYTHS
JIM DAVIS

HAVE A FISH, GARFIELD
JIM DAVIS
GULP
PTOOEY
© 1980 United Feature Syndicate, Inc.
3-23
THAT WAS AMAZING!
I HAVE NIMBLE TEETH

GUESS WHAT, GARFIELD? I'M ENTERING YOU IN A CAT SHOW
3-24
© 1980 United Feature Syndicate, Inc.

THAT SHOULD BE FUN...

I'LL BE DYNAMITE IN THE SWIMSUIT COMPETITION
JIM DAVIS

YOU'LL HAVE TO TAKE A BATH BEFORE THE CAT SHOW, GARFIELD
I'LL TAKE MY CHANCES
3-25

CLEAN CATS ARE WINNING CATS

THE THINGS I DO FOR STARDOM
© 1980 United Feature Syndicate, Inc.
JIM DAVIS

NOW LET'S FLUFF YOU UP
3-26

RRRRRR

© 1980 United Feature Syndicate, Inc.
JIM DAVIS

WE NEED A GIMMICK FOR THE CAT SHOW, GARFIELD, SOMETHING TO MAKE THE JUDGE NOTICE YOU
3-27

THIS SHOULD DO IT

IT'S A SAD STATE OF AFFAIRS WHEN A PET OWNER STOOPS TO HUMILIATING A CAT
JIM DAVIS
© 1980 United Feature Syndicate, Inc.

THEY'LL PROBABLY WANT YOU TO DO TRICKS AT THE CAT SHOW, GARFIELD. SO HOP THROUGH THIS HOOP

3-28

I COULD JUST CRY
JIM DAVIS
© 1980 United Feature Syndicate, Inc.

HURRY UP, GARFIELD! TIME TO LEAVE FOR THE CAT SHOW
GRRR
ROWR
© 1980 United Feature Syndicate, Inc.
3-29

YIP! ROWR! FFT!

I COULD JUST CRY
JIM DAVIS

© 1980 United Feature Syndicate, Inc.

Garfield Up Close and Personal

Q: What is your favorite sport?
A: *Each morning, before breakfast, I like to take a good, brisk nap.*

Q: Where did you get your nasty temper, and why are you so cynical?
A: *Step a little closer and ask that.*

Q: Describe your relationship with Jon, Odie, Pooky, and Nermal.
A: *Someone to abuse, someone to pound on, someone to confide in, and no comment.*

Q: Why did you call your most recent book "GARFIELD Bigger Than Life"?
A: *I didn't name the book, actually. I have the distinct feeling it is some kind of slur on my size. The book was named by my late editor.*

Q: How much money did you get for this book?
A: *Heavens to Betsy, I'm just a cat. That sort of thing doesn't concern me. Ask my agent.*

Q: Now that you are a success, do you give yourself your own baths?
A: *No, I've hired a cat to take baths for me.*

Q: Are you a prima donna?
A: *Not really.*

Q: Is there anyone with whom you would like to share the credit for your success?
A: *Not really.*